SOLAR ECLIPSE

WINNING OUR WAR

BETWEEN

LIGHT AND DARKNESS

SOULAR ECLIPSE

WINNING OUR WAR
BETWEEN
LIGHT AND DARKNESS

GLENN GOREE

eLectio Publishing
Little Elm, TX
www.eLectioPublishing.com

Soular Eclipse: Winning Our War Between Light and Darkness
By Glenn Goree

Copyright 2014 by Glenn Goree
Cover Design by eLectio Publishing, LLC

ISBN-13: 978-1-63213-036-5
Published by eLectio Publishing, LLC
Little Elm, Texas
http://www.eLectioPublishing.com

Printed in the United States of America

Scripture taken from the HOLY BIBLE, NEW INTERNATIONAL VERSION®. NIV®. Copyright © 1973, 1978 by International Bible Society. Used by permission of Zondervan. All rights reserved worldwide.

Without limiting the rights under copyright reserved above, no part of this publication may be reproduced, stored in or introduced into a retrieval system, or transmitted, in any form, or by any means (electronic, mechanical, photocopying, recording, or otherwise), without the prior written permission of both the copyright owner and the above publisher of this book.

If you purchased this book without a cover, you should be aware that this book is stolen property. It was reported as "unsold and destroyed" to the publisher and neither the author nor the publisher has received any payment for the "stripped book."

The scanning, uploading, and distribution of this book via the Internet or via any other means without the permission of the publisher is illegal and punishable by law. Please purchase only authorized electronic editions, and do not participate in or encourage electronic piracy of copyrighted materials. Your support of the author's rights is appreciated.

Publisher's Note
The publisher does not have any control over and does not assume any responsibility for author or third-party websites or their content.

I dedicate this book to my bride of forty-two years,
Valerie Goree,
Without whom my life would be incomplete.

CONTENTS

Introduction 1

ONE
The Virulence of Hate 19

TWO
Insecurity by Another Name 25

THREE
Seven Lessons of How to Live in the Light and Avoid the Darkness ... 31

FOUR
Three Reasons We Choose to Live in the Darkness 39

FIVE
The Triangle of Light: Making the Light Your Home 49

SIX
Can We Really Know Another's Darkness: Inclusive and Exclusive Darkness 55

SEVEN
Transcending Darkness: How to Understand Another's Darkness 61

EIGHT
Sharing Light and Darkness: How to Help during Dark Times 67

NINE
Questions about Our Own Darkness 73

TEN
Merry-Go-Round of Darkness 75

"Many are asking, 'Who can show us any good?' Let the light of your face shine upon us, O Lord. You have filled my heart with greater joy than when their grain and new wine abound." (Psalm 4:6-7)

"The lamp of the Lord searches the spirit of a man; it searches out his inmost being." (Proverb 20:27)

Introduction

It was a typical morning at one of the locations where I provide counseling. I love my job as an Employee Assistance Program (EAP) counselor. After seven years, it feels more like a family than a company. The boss to whom I report for this contract told me when I started that being the on-site counselor is like being the chaplain on an aircraft carrier. He was absolutely right.

On this particular morning I returned from one of our break rooms with a cup of morning coffee and saw an employee who had a history of cancer. I knew he'd had an outpatient procedure to remove the cancer, and he had been released by his doctor to return to work. He'd been cancer free for nearly a year and was so thankful, and then during a routine checkup a few weeks ago, the doctor discovered the cancer had returned. This was his second bout with cancer!

I asked how he was, and I could tell from his downcast expression there was no cause for celebration this morning. He reported that while he was in surgery after the new discovery from his last follow-up visit, the doctor had done a full-body scan and had discovered cancer in his left lung. Plans had been made to remove this spot at a later date. I asked if he would like to have a prayer together. He agreed, so we went to my office, closed the door, and prayed for the upcoming surgery on his lung.

After he left, I closed the door again and wept uncontrollably. I composed myself after fifteen minutes and went about my day. Normally I don't cry over this type of situation because I hear cases like his every week. The difference between his case and others was that, just a few days before, I had counseled a woman with another tragic story.

It seems she was dealing with Post-Traumatic Stress Disorder (PTSD). Two years before our meeting, she had been tracked down by her husband. She had left him after ten years of marriage because of his physical abuse, but when he found her he demanded she return home with their nine-year-old daughter. When she insisted their marriage was over, he pulled out a pistol from a bag he was carrying and shot her eight times. He placed four bullets in the back of each of her legs, just above the knees. As she lay on the floor, losing consciousness, she heard two more shots. Later, when she woke up in the hospital, she learned he had fatally shot their preadolescent daughter and had then turned the pistol on himself.

As though murder and suicide were not enough, he also left a note. It stated he did not intend for her to die. He wanted to leave her paralyzed so she would know what it was like to be alive and not have their daughter or be able to have a relationship with another man. Though she survived and her body healed—she was able to walk in spite of the odds against it—her question to me was, how could she pick up the shattered pieces of her life?

Just a few days prior to hearing this poor lady's sad story, I encountered another female employee who was seeking help because her husband had an addiction to pornography. I cannot relay the details here because it was one of the worst scenarios I have heard in decades. What he did was so disgusting and vile that the memory of her story causes me to be repulsed.

I think you can see what led to my tears. Looking back now, I realize it was not that these situations were new. I'd been in private practice for many years and had heard other gut-wrenching stories. I think it was not only the nature of these situations but the accumulation of the three events so close together.

The human psyche, no matter how well trained and experienced to help wounded souls, sometimes reaches its limits. And mine was beyond its breach. The tears I shed did help, but they were only a temporary fix. All day long I functioned as though I were impervious to the burden of these stories of bruised and battered souls.

As I was traveling home that night, these life events repeated themselves in my head and demonstrated just how cruel the darkness in life can be to its victims. It is deep, dank, and sinister. It knows no boundaries and equally assaults man, woman, and child. Darkness gives no quarter and seeks unbridled punishment with a vengeance. It surrounds us all throughout our lives and sometimes takes life before leaving the womb. We are not aware of this darkness as we are growing up from infancy, but it seeks to devour us when we begin to leave the protection of our parents. Then, as we explore life on our own, the menace is there to embrace us as a villain waiting to steal our souls.

There are two types of darkness that are entwined in our lives. First, there is the darkness of the external world in which we live and breathe. Second, there is darkness from within our hearts.

The External Darkness

I find it interesting that we continue each day as though nothing were wrong in our lives while, in reality, we live in external darkness. My mind returned to some of my casual greetings at work. Did that lady I just passed and exchanged hellos with experience the darkness of spousal abuse last night or this morning? Why is she wearing long sleeves on a hot day like this? Could it be she is hiding something?

An oncoming vehicle's lights flashed in my eyes, and I pondered how we can deal sanely with so much darkness in this world. The darkness rolls over all in its path like a tsunami, engulfing, overpowering, and refusing to release its grip. Each person I attempt to help has his or her own unique external darkness. And as a matter of fact, I have my own external darkness that surrounds me each day. At times I have found myself unable to cope with it.

External Darkness: Shared and Unique

I then realized that we all share external darkness in unique yet simultaneous experiences. For example, Americans are now facing terrorism in our homeland—something much of the world has experienced for thirty years or more. When it happens on our soil, we do not share the exact same external darkness that much of the world has. Since September 11, 2001, we know to some extent what it is like to lose loved ones to terrorism; however, one major difference is that

American civilians have not had to protect their own homes and fight terrorists firsthand.

Americans have not had to band together in small groups and develop counter-insurgency strategies to protect their children. In general, civilians have not faced ambushes or kidnappings or had to place sandbags on the floors of their cars in case they hit a land mine. They don't have to patrol their properties in either rural or urban communities, and they don't have to examine their homes from the standpoint of possible homestead attacks, developing strategies to guard their homes against AK-47 rifles or rocket-propelled grenades (RPGs). So yes, we do share a common external darkness but not in the same way.

External Darkness: Individual Experience

Even though this darkness is shared, it becomes unique to the experience of each individual; hence, we cannot understand each other's external darkness or how the other person experiences it. For example, there is an image burned into my memory from 1976. I see the event just as clearly today as I did then, many decades ago.

My wife Valerie and I had been on a Christian mission in southern Africa for about a year when terrorists moved into the farmland district surrounding where we lived. The twelve farms of our quadrant held a meeting to map out how to communicate and how to protect against terrorist attack on individual homes. We called this meeting a *laager*, which is an Afrikaans term we Americans would express as "circle the wagons."

An interesting side note is that the Afrikaans pioneers piled thorn bushes called "wag-'n-bietjie bos," which literally translates to "wait a minute bush," in large clusters filling the gaps between the wagons. They were called "wait a minute bushes" because once the thorns pierced the skin the experience quickly became like falling into barbed wire.

The terrorists were fond of attacking at night. Usually they could walk freely around a farm or our mission because they were in civilian clothes. They could accomplish this incognito reconnaissance because they blended in with the workers. After a few days of surveillance, they learned the routines which made their victims vulnerable at identified weak points of defense. It is during these strategic times that they would plan an ambush.

Consequently, my wife and I studied our own personal daily routines and tried to be prepared for whatever might come our way. At night, just before dusk, we put coarse black cloths over our windows because the terrorists liked to shoot civilians through their exposed, clear windows. Visible house lights indicated which rooms were occupied and showed silhouetted occupants moving from room to room. The whole house was constructed from thick adobe bricks, and a long hallway connected all of the bedrooms. Each night we would roll our daughter's baby carriage into the hall so she would have two windowless walls for protection. In the morning, we'd roll the carriage back into her room where she'd sleep in her crib during the day.

We had a good reason for executing this charade. To earn money, mission school children would work in our house, and we knew there was a strong likelihood that they would inform the terrorist group where we slept. By waiting until after dark to move our daughter's carriage to the hall, the terrorists did not know of her new location. If they fired an RPG at her window, they would hit an empty room. My wife and I also used this strategy by making the bed in the spare room look as though we'd slept there instead of in the master bedroom.

Like a well-trained soldier, each night I would clean and load my FN automatic rifle that shot 7.62 mm armor-piercing rounds. I never slid one into the chamber but loaded a full magazine in the rifle with the safety on. I kept the rifle on the floor parallel to my side of the bed, which was closest to the large panoramic window into which terrorists could shoot their AK-47 rifles or fire RPGs. Our strategy was for Valerie to roll off onto the floor, keeping the bed between her and the window, and then crawl into the hall to our baby daughter.

Several years later, after we left the mission, I learned of a personal decision my wife had made. She did not want to have a second baby while we still lived at the mission. At the time I could not comprehend her procrastination because we wanted to have two children that were close together in age. She later explained that as the security situation deteriorated, she had envisioned a strong possibility of being forced to run for safety. She could do this much more easily with only one child to care for. There were many occasions when I was not there to protect her if necessary, so if faced with this dilemma, she would have been by herself.

Living under the weight of this psychological strain day in and day out eventually became a burden. In some ways, though, it was a challenge to see how we could outsmart our adversaries in this cat-and-mouse contest. Everyday life continued as though there were no concerns in the world except living life to its fullest. Weeks passed, months passed, and nothing happened. In time these daily routines against counter-insurgency become the norm.

Geese and ducks in yards around houses were not the exotic window dressing of genteel country living but prompt and very loud alarm systems against intruders. They made more noise and provided better warning signals than dogs. I also learned by bitter humorous experience that ducks and geese are fearless and even more territorial than dogs. And they don't roll over to have their tummies scratched.

Another part of the daily routine was participating in tracking exercises; our neighbor taught me how to look for spores, travel nimbly, and cross open spaces until all became commonplace. Our first introduction to the seriousness of what can happen in this lifestyle was when we were woken early one morning with a surprise knock at our back door. The local military were conducting a spontaneous visit to see if we were hiding terrorists. After all, they saw the same tracks on the mission as they discovered on the local farms and knew that terrorists were freely moving, so why wouldn't they suspect we were hiding them?

It became second nature to drive outside of the gravel road ruts because these ruts were often where the terrorists would plant land mines. They knew traffic tended to stay in these well-worn ruts because even during these war days local travelers would become complacent. Another common sight on the road was piles of cow dung; it was better not to tempt fate by driving over them. They were often used as camouflage to cover a strategically placed land mine that would definitely turn a good day into a bad one. One final routine was to inspect the dirt road leading up to our house each morning. We never knew if perhaps the night before a land mine had been planted. This was a common trick the terrorists used, and they had been successful in murdering several local farmers.

Living under this stress for not just months but years can take its emotional toll on even the most stout-hearted individual. After several months we heard that one farmer in our district had "packed it in," which is a Rhodesian idiom meaning that his family could no longer take the daily strain of never knowing when or how they would be ambushed by the terrorists, and moved away.

To minimize the potential danger, some families sent their children to boarding school in the cities. Others with small children lived day to day and avidly followed the reports of attacks on other farms. No one thought ill of those families who left. We all respected each other and recognized the personal decision each family had to make based on their individual circumstances.

Oddly enough, war makes strange bedfellows and can create humorous situations. Once I met a German who had been a soldier in the German army in World War II. At the conclusion of the war, he'd immigrated to Rhodesia, a land that offered him a new start in life. When he heard my American accent, he could not help but make a comment. "Hey, I fought you during World War Two and now we are on the same side." I smiled in agreement, but I never saw him again.

A similar event occurred after the terrorist war in Rhodesia had ended. I worked for a major corporation in their Human Resources Department. I was in Salisbury, the capital, recruiting for the organization. They had provided a list of possible candidates to screen and, as it turned out, one day I interviewed two ex-terrorists.

Both men were from the MaShona tribe in Rhodesia and had been recruited by the Communists during the war and trained to be insurgents. One was trained in Russia and the other in China. Now that the war was over, they needed jobs like everybody else. It was strange to sit before two young men about my age when only months before we'd been trying to kill each other. They were strangers to me, but I would have killed them both without hesitation if I'd met them in the bush in previous years. As the saying goes, "Nothing personal, just following my orders." But I didn't hate them. Had these men been hired by the company, we could have worked together and become friends. We may have had meals together at each other's homes. Our kids could have played together, never knowing that their fathers were enemies at one time. Our wives could have become friends and ganged up on us like women do in the ongoing husband-and-wife competition.

External darkness does have its cruel little ironies.

Every so often during the war, we would receive word that a terrorist accidentally blew himself up while trying to set a land mine in the road. We would celebrate, laugh, and joke about his death. One less terrorist to kill, we would say among other epitaphs of cold, hard indifference. Looking back now, I wonder if one of those men who blew himself up was a brother, cousin, or uncle of the two young men I interviewed? How would I feel about the death if it was a relative of a man I knew?

On another occasion I watched two doctors allow a terrorist to die when they could have saved him. I chanced upon the area where this terrorist lay on the ground, gasping for breath while the two doctors stood over him snickering. It was a joke to them. Watching him die was no different than stepping on a bug. I made no comment because I was only a medic and these men were doctors.

I experienced still more twisted irony when one bright day I visited a farmer and vacated my truck in his front yard to go greet him. Out of the corner of my eye, I saw a huge dark four-legged beast that resembled a wolf charging in my direction. He was not coming to say howdy. One look at his face and I jumped back into my truck so fast I probably broke some land-speed record. The farmer pulled his dog off my vehicle and chained him up so I could get out and visit. He explained that this animal's training as a watchdog either backfired or did not take. He'd been trained to guard against transient black tribal Africans. Somehow the message did not get through and the dog literally hated any and every white Anglo-Saxon male but loved the local tribal Africans.

Internal Darkness

As I said earlier in the introduction, I have an image burned in my memory from about 1976. You probably think by now it's some grisly image of death or some horror of having been in a firefight with terrorists at the mission. No. This image is nothing like that. It is far more horrifying, far worse than some story of blood and guts. It's the image of a young mother in her mid to late thirties and her son, about ten to twelve. She is in a casual dress, something a woman would wear on a farm or ranch. Around her slim waist she wears a belt and holster carrying a large pistol. Just like in the Old West, a line of bullets is neatly tucked in slots along the back of the belt.

Standing next to her is her son, dressed in khaki shorts and a T-shirt and looking much older than his preadolescent years because he is brandishing a twelve-gauge shotgun. He is not handling the weapon like an excited kid whose parents just let him hold it. No. He is handling it like an old pro. He displays the shotgun like someone accustomed to the weapon, like it's a part of his daily life and has been for a long time. There is no showmanship, no braggadocio, no attitude of, "See what I got?" He's not even a teen, and he already knows what it means to face death each day. He has probably never kissed a woman other than his mother and yet he is considered a valued asset in case a firefight breaks out.

Sadder still, what if he is in a firefight and is killed? He would have his life cut short and would have never known the love of a good woman. He'd never get to hold a newborn son or daughter nor have the thrill of carving out a life and future for his family. He would never see his children grow up and watch them graduate from school, get married, and have children of their own.

But there is something even more horrifying than his losing his life. What if he's forced to kill? What if, in the course of defending his home, he shoots and kills another human being? Even if you take into consideration that war requires a "kill or be killed" attitude, the burden of death exists. It's difficult enough for a soldier to fight and kill in war, but he's only a boy. How could he carry this internal darkness for the rest of his life?

How does this boy fall asleep at night when the dark image of the face of the man or men he has killed is burned into his memory? To whom does he cry out in terror? Where can he seek solace? He's a man now, and men hide their pain. They don't share it. How can he assuage his guilt? From whom can he seek forgiveness when he cannot forgive himself? After all, he has nothing for which to be forgiven; he was just doing his duty. Did he ever accept his actions as something he had to do and not something he wanted to do?

Why is this so upsetting, you might ask? It's because almost every other mother and son of this age was dressed and equipped in the same manner. Everyone had a weapon of some sort. Carrying it was as much a part of daily life as brushing teeth or putting on shoes. These weapons were not for show. They were necessities for survival, not ornaments or signs of frivolity. They could mean the difference between a child dying or staying alive, a spouse becoming a widower or staying married, or a family staying intact or being scattered across a battlefield. Carrying weapons was serious business where all participants were playing for keeps.

Here is another reason why this scene is indelibly sketched in my memory: the internal darkness every person lived with each day. The external darkness of war had created an internal darkness that each person shared. However, this internal menace was still unique to each individual—my wife and I included. Living in this internal darkness with our own peculiar responses to the external darkness was a stress only those experiencing it could grasp. And yet, though we were one with each other, there was no way each of us could grasp how the other felt, even when we attempted to transcend our shared internal and external darkness.

I believe the closest we as a community came to sharing our internal darkness happened after a terrorist attack on a local farmstead.

Internal Darkness: Shared and Unique

My wife and I decided to have a series of five Sundays devoted to collective worship regardless of religious background. Our theme was asking God to bring peace to our community and an end to the war. The meetings were held at the community clubhouse and recreation center. Since the residents lived in remote areas, the clubhouse served as a gathering place where the farmers and ranchers could get together on weekends for fellowship. We were not sure how many would show up each week because I personally didn't know how many farms and ranches were in the district beyond the mission.

The first Sunday we had about twenty souls for the worship service, which was twenty more than I thought would show up. However, between the first and second week, one of the farms was attacked. Thankfully no one was killed, but the incident put the fear of God in us all.

I visited the farmer the day after the attack and he explained what had happened. God must have been looking out for his family. They had a very large old tree in front of one of the entrances to their house where the main attack occurred. An RPG had been fired at the entrance but hit the tree and exploded. If the rocket had made a direct hit on the house, the outcome would have been very different.

For the second Sunday service, we prepared for about twenty people but at least fifty showed up. We had to secure chairs stored in a back room, dusty from lack of use, to make rows for people to sit, but even then some men had to stand in the back of the room, as there was standing room only.

A different atmosphere filled this service compared to the previous week. I'm not sure how to explain it. The singing was certainly more enthusiastic, no matter how off-key, but as I think through the event now, the difference was in the expressions on the faces of these farmers and ranchers.

Where they afraid? Sure. Where they all thankful no one was killed? You bet. But I sensed more than these natural responses to the threat of death. I think the people there were united by a common internal darkness. Though only one family had been attacked, each family shared in their darkness of a common mortality.

Internal Darkness: Individual Experience

After two years, my wife and I decided to leave the mission. Looking back, I'm not sure what was in my internal darkness that led to this decision. Could it have been that late night we heard movement outside our house? At this point I need to add that we did not have a telephone, so we could not communicate with other residents on the mission and were somewhat isolated in our home's location. I don't remember the details of every action we took, but I do recall we ensured all the windows were covered, our daughter was safely in the hallway, and the lights were out. Rifle in hand, first I peeked out a window at the back of the house and saw no movement. Then I did the same at the living room window. Again, no movement, but we continued to hear noises like someone moving and stopping, walking through the tall, dry grass. Finally I went to the kitchen door and cracked it just a bit. In the moonlight I saw several head of cattle ambling through our yard.

Apparently, the cattle had escaped their pen and were grazing freely in the open field, moving from one grassy area to another. How can I explain my relief? It was as though I had every bit of energy drained out of my body. I now knew from firsthand experience the flight fight mechanism. It was no longer a psychological term I learned in graduate school, but a stark fear in reality to master in potential confrontation of life and death. I felt exhausted at the end of those several minutes in determining what if any potential danger existed. My wife and I both laughed as a form of comic relief and I realized the laughter replaced tears of joy and thanksgiving.

Another reason we chose to leave the mission could have been what happened to a young couple we befriended. They lived on a farm next to the mission and were attacked but survived. We learned that the terrorists set their tobacco barns on fire and ran off all their field hands. There was a brief exchange of fire and the terrorists retreated.

Or maybe it was the night the secondary school headmaster's house burned up like a Roman candle. Fellow mission residents tried to rescue his furniture and other possessions but were unsuccessful. No one was hurt, but I will never forget either the enormous flames that seemed to burn clear up to the stars or the heat they generated. We had neither water hoses nor a water supply from the mission's water tank, so we formed a bucket brigade. These feeble attempts were like throwing tubs of aspirins into a cancer and hoping some miracle would transpire.

Maybe our decision was influenced by the dusk-to-dawn curfew imposed on our area. I don't really know. What I do know is that my internal darkness was building at a progressive rate. How was I to protect my wife and daughter? Could I really justify going off all day on Sunday to preach in the villages, leaving my family behind in the mission? They were alone and had no one there to protect them.

I never did learn why two African youths came to our house while I was gone one Sunday and told my wife I was needed out in a field.

When I returned that evening we could not locate these two youths, nor could we understand their request for me to venture into some remote field when I had nothing to do with the agricultural program. Could it have been a trap set to murder me? We asked around and could not find any one on the mission who knew or admitted to knowing who these boys were and why they asked for me.

Life under these circumstances begins to wear on you. Your personality starts to change. Trust is replaced with doubt and suspicion. Innocence is replaced with skepticism. Faith starts to demand proof, and performing good deeds starts to require a questioning of motive and hidden agenda. By this time, neither of us was the idealistic missionary who had originally arrived on the mission. Doubt and suspicion became the order of the day. And in spite of all these bits and pieces forming the mosaic of our internal darkness, there was one that stood out the most.

It was hate.

"The people walking in darkness have seen a great light; on those living in the land of darkness a light has dawned." (Isaiah 9:2)

"...Giving thanks to the Father, who has qualified you to share in the inheritance of the saints in the kingdom of light. For he has rescued us from the dominion of darkness and brought us in the kingdom of the Son he loves, in whom we have redemption, the forgiveness of sins." (Colossians 1:12-14)

ONE
The Virulence of Hate

About two years after we moved to Bulawayo, I got a job working for a major retail company in their Human Resources Department. I was their recruitment and career development officer. It was a very exciting job. I was blessed to rub elbows with people from all over the world, for Rhodesia, like America, had been a melting pot of global proportion since the end of World War II.

Our chief of human resources was from the MaShona tribe in Rhodesia. He had started with the company pushing a broom and then worked his way up through the ranks. He was a very nice man, genteel and friendly, and he worked well with everyone. He was thoroughly westernized as he had a monogamous marriage and several children. Sadly, I never got the opportunity to meet his family.

It was within this corporate environment and Human Resources Department that I learned about the virulence of hate—because I was chronically infected.

Like most viruses, one never knows of its bodily inhabitance until signs and symptoms emerge. My symptoms were manifest in my relationship with the chief of our Human Resources Department. They became self-evident one day when my boss asked me in a memo to do some work for him. My ego was already the size of Texas by the time I had worked in my new job for several months. My immature reasoning was, "Why am I working as a subordinate to a man who has no formal education when I possess a master's degree?" These thoughts were the first signs of my denial of the virus of hate. Like most people with a medical viral condition, when first diagnosed I chose to pretend it didn't exist.

I later tersely responded with a memo to my boss, writing that if he wanted to get these tasks done, then he needed to do them himself. I refused to carry him any longer with my expertise. You can easily see that more symptoms of hate had raised their ugly, viral heads.

A few days went by and I never had a reply from my boss, so I figured everything was fine. I had set him straight about how important I was and how fortunate he was to have hired me. I was on top of the world. He may be the official boss, but everyone knew, including my mentor, who had a bachelor's degree, that I was really in charge. After all, though I had been with the company for only about six months, I knew more than this black African did and a little more than my white female mentor.

My false piety along with my "deep" humility fooled no one except myself. These were still more symptoms of soul-stealing hate. However, I could mask them with determination and sterling performance so that no one could challenge me to take a good, hard look at myself. Sometime during this hypocritical end-zone victory dance, the hate virus fully infected my heart and soul. It circulated without encumbrance through the spiritual bloodstream of my now darkly porous conscience. I don't know how to describe it, but the weight of my own words, thoughts, and actions came lumbering down on my spirit. They fell so hard I went into a deep depression.

What had happened to me? From where did all this hate emerge? It had crept in so slowly yet deliberately. I realized I had purposefully chosen not to acknowledge it, so it became comfortable in its newfound home. It subtly numbed my conscience one small piece at a time until it ultimately triumphed, chasing out all moral conscience from within.

Looking back nearly thirty years later, I saw that the two years on the mission had slowly converted my heart. Terrorism had taken its toll on my emotional and mental balance. It had tipped the scales of fair and just thinking toward severe racial prejudice.

I don't recall what finally forced me to face the hate that had consumed me. It could have been a word from my corporate mentor, my wife's purity, guilt struggling to hang on by a fingertip, or perhaps all of these. But one day I finally faced the fact that hate filled my heart.

Like the Apostle Paul said in the New Testament after his conversion, "something like scales" fell from his eyes, and he could see again! So, too, had something fallen from my eyes and allowed me to see how I let hate rule my life. My moral trespass was not the insubordination toward my boss; no, this was only one of many viral hate symptoms. My sin was against God and not man.

My only course of action was to go to my boss and ask for his forgiveness. So a few days later we had a private meeting. While waiting for our scheduled meeting, I sat down and wrote out a list of my sins. I then prayed over them, asking for God's forgiveness. I had to seek His forgiveness first, for I realized I was like the prodigal son in the New Testament book of Luke (Chapter 15).

Prayer prepared the way for our meeting and also laid the foundation for a lasting friendship. I showed my list of sins to my boss and asked for his forgiveness. He graciously accepted my request and extended his forgiveness. We shook hands at the end of our meeting before returning to our respective work stations, and I cannot begin to express the load of guilt that was lifted from my heart. For the first time in a year I saw life through the light. My spiritual life had returned, only better. My marriage improved and I had a better outlook on life as a whole.

These changes were only the beginning. My boss and I quickly became close friends, and I learned how to hold hands with him in public. This act was the custom in his culture when two men were more than coworkers and colleagues. It was a little awkward at first, but I quickly became adept at knowing when to hold his hand.

Something else emerged a few months later. One day I asked my boss a question that had been bothering me. Why had he not fired me for insubordination? His reply proved another example of God turning a bad situation into something good. He told me, "Glenn, you are the first white man in my life who has apologized to me." You could have knocked me down with a feather. I thought to myself, he is about thirty-five and in all his life no white man has ever apologized to him?

How did he not become bitter? How had he not allowed racial prejudice to infect him as severely as it had infected me? He was truly a better man than I! His lesson in patience inspired me.

The defeat of my viral hatred through the power of God's Holy Spirit taught me some valuable lessons about His light. I would like to share them with you here.

First, the light is independent of its recipients. It does not depend on those who live in it, nor does it ask for admittance, but once invited into the darkness there is no stopping it. Second, it knows neither limits nor boundaries. Yet, in spite of all its power, if we are not careful we can slip into the darkness again and the light will not try to stop us. Third, it only goes where it is invited and requested to live. The light cannot be induced, courted, or coached. Fourth, it has its own mission and purpose independent of its host and does not deviate from it because it is no respecter of persons. Fifth, unlike us, it is true, honest, and sincere. It does not play games or have hidden agendas. Sixth, the light is pure, reliable, and dependable so that if we chose to live in its strength, it will always be there in our lives. Seventh, it will never give up on us and will always hope, persevere, and be true to its nature. Finally, light cannot possibly change or exist any other way.

"This is the message we have heard from him and declare to you: God is light; in him there is no darkness at all. If we claim to have fellowship with him yet walk in the darkness, we lie and do not live by the truth. But if we walk in the light, as he is in the light, we have fellowship with one another, and the blood of Jesus, his Son, purifies us from all sin." (I John 1: 5-7)

TWO
Insecurity by Another Name

Darkness Where Least Expected

Several years ago I counseled a young nurse who returned from the Middle East with classic symptoms of PTSD. In the course of her therapy she related several stories of the war between her light and darkness. One of the worst stories she shared was about a young Muslim boy of about ten or eleven. He was brought into the hospital where she worked after having stepped on a land mine, and he was so severely wounded that the medical personnel weren't sure he would survive. From the nurse's description, the patient was held together with tape, tubes, and sutures. He received blood transfusions for several days due to the excessive blood loss.

Surprising everyone, he slowly but surely began to make progress. Once he was stable and hastily patched together, his parents were allowed to visit him for short periods of time. After a few months, the boy was ready to return home. The nurses, who worked on him as though he was their own child, gathered extra medicine, bandages, and other medical supplies for his family to take home.

This hospital was surrounded by a wall with sentries at the gates and along the perimeter. Guards were fully armed with automatic weapons twenty-four hours a day. Sentries manned the main gate while they observed the reunion of this boy with his parents.

Not a movement was made that was not under the meticulous scrutiny of these guards for every second the family reunion continued. The nurses turned around, feeling a tremendous burden had been relieved from their shoulders after this six-month ordeal. They had their backs to the boy and his family as they were walking in the courtyard, returning to the hospital, and simultaneously the boy and his family were departing away from the gate to the outside community.

Suddenly, the nurses heard a loud explosion and ducked. Then the guards barked orders and aimed their weapons at the family. The nurses turned to see that the family had walked a distance from the gate before the father had pulled out a pistol and shot the boy in the head. He was murdered within minutes of discharge from the hospital.

The nurses couldn't leave the safety of the hospital no matter how badly they wanted to come to the boy's aid. If they had left the compound, there was no promise of their wellbeing. You can imagine the terror they felt after having witnessed this senseless act of violence.

It made no sense to these nurses, but shooting this boy in the head made perfect sense to his family. They were poor and had barely enough to eat. Although they loved their son, he would have been a financial drain on the family. The father's decision to murder his son was an economic choice, weighing the value of one against the welfare of many. It made sense to him, no matter what westerners thought.

Let me ask some questions that immediately come to mind. Regardless of the cultural norms, how does a father murder his own son? Wouldn't any dad search for some way to care for his son, no matter what obstacles came along? Did this boy expect to be shot? Was he amazed that his family actually came to take him home and care for him? Could it be that perhaps he expected to be shot all along? In his short life he'd probably witnessed similar decisions made under dire circumstances.

How could a father live with the internal darkness of taking his own son's life even after the boy had survived other tragedies? I wondered if only this man committed this terminal act or if any father in the peasantry of the Muslim world would have had the same value system. I learned from my client that this was the norm, because it was not the only case. In several other circumstances, families of wounded civilians were given medicine and, instead of using it to aid in healing, it was sold to buy food.

One veterinarian, for example, treated a family's mule because the animal was overloaded for an extended period of time. This uncaring practice resulted in the mule's hide being worn down to the exposure of muscle and bone. The doctor faithfully applied medication and instructed the family to let the mule rest until its back healed. He also gave them medicine and bandages, which they promptly sold to purchase food. The next day the veterinarian saw the mule with an enormous burden on its bare flesh.

What Is Insecurity?

I went to the Middle East once for several weeks to provide grief counseling. Prior to my arrival, Taliban terrorists had killed a number of employees of an expatriate corporation.

I counseled several Muslim employees of different ages and educations, and nearly every one of them asked the same question in separate interviews: "How do I overcome insecurity?" Automatically, my answer formed around what a typical American would do to feel secure—change in yourself what you feel insecure about. Set new goals. Go back to school. Get more exercise and rest, and change your diet.

At the end of each of these sessions I got the same blank stare. It was like, "Hey Glenn, you completely missed the boat! You didn't listen to what I asked. How do I escape this constant insecurity?" These employees were too polite to tell me up front that I did not grasp what they were really asking. Instead each one respectfully concluded our session and departed, thanking me very much for how I had helped them. However, I knew something was wrong because they were being too polite, but I could not identify the reason.

Upon reflection, I realized that once they had posed their question I should have asked, "What does insecurity mean to you?" In the third session, I realized by the employee's reply how foolish I had been.

In the following paragraphs you will read a composite story of what these young and old employees had accepted as their unique way of life. I could not take notes at the time because in this type of counseling it is not the accepted practice, so what I am about to relate is from the best of my memory. Though I may miss a few details, I will never forget the tragedy of what a whole generation of people had lived through from cradle to grave. The darkness they experienced with the Taliban extends beyond anything a person of any faith can accept as normal religious behavior, no matter how much one may wish to respect another faith.

What is insecurity? In their own words, it was the uncertainty of not knowing if when they said good-bye to their families in the morning as they all left home for school and work they would see each other that evening. At any time, any of them could be arrested and taken away by the Taliban-controlled police, never to be seen again. Their external darkness was having the "morals police" constantly patrol neighborhoods. Any girl could be arrested at random for dressing immodestly and taken away or beaten, sometimes to death, on the spot.

One particular story I heard was about a man's uncle who was pulled out of his house, beaten, and left in the street for reasons only known to the morals police of the Taliban. His family could not attend to his wounds because they feared retaliation. I can't recall the details, but I think in this instance the family waited until the early morning hours to attend to the body. There were also stories of people beaten in the streets, set on fire, and left to burn to death.

One young girl in her twenties told me her story of determination. It seems girls were not permitted to learn to read, much less receive an education. If a girl was found with a book, the Taliban declared her and her family traitors and killed them. Traitors to what, I thought? Why is a girl reading a book thought of as being traitorous? Did the Taliban think that if girls dared to become educated they would question ancient superstitions? Was the Taliban fearful of change in their society's role for women?

This young woman led an underground movement where books were smuggled into a different home on different days. The young girls gathered in these homes, careful not to draw attention to themselves, and here they read and studied together. The girls continued this practice for more than a year even though they knew what they were doing was punishable by death.

"Do not gloat over me, my enemy! Though I have fallen, I will rise. Though I sit in darkness, the Lord will be my light." (Micah 7:8)

"For with you is the fountain of life; in your light we see light." (Psalm 36:9)

THREE
Seven Lessons of How to Live in the Light and Avoid the Darkness

Dawn of Darkness: First Awareness

Let me ask you some questions. Can you recall the first time you were afraid? Do you remember where you were and why you were fearful? Was your fear assuaged? If so, how? Who rescued you from this first experience of darkness, or fear? I deliberately use the word darkness because it describes the experience of a fear of the unknown.

Although I'm not a doctor, I've worked with the chronically mentally ill for decades. I believe this darkness plays a significant role in their mental illness regardless of the illness's form, type, or cause. Madness may be the stuff of mental illness, but darkness is the stuff or our madness.

Relationships of all kinds suffer from this darkness. Marriages crumble, friendships falter, businesses collapse, communities cave, nations fall, and, from a Christian perspective, souls are lost. I think these events can all be traced back to how we as individuals confronted the internal darkness that was formed by the external darkness in which we live. I believe it is how we answered the call of this first encounter with darkness that forms a pattern in our lives. Let me give you a personal example.

One night when I was a young boy of seven or eight, I awoke with an intense fear. I don't know its origin or why it occurred. I started crying and ran into my dad's office, where he slept sometimes after working late. It was a hot summer night in Houston, Texas, and the air was thick with humidity—so thick I probably could have held a glass up and waited for the water to fall out of the air and fill it.

I remember running to my dad's bed and waking him. He asked what had frightened me, and I told him between sobs that I was afraid of dying. He laughed sympathetically, attempting to reduce the tension of my fear. He told me not to worry and allowed me to crawl into bed with him. My dad had been an eighteen-year-old marine in the Fourth Marine Division in World War II and was part of the invasion of Saipan and Tinian. He'd often faced this question of dying. In my entire life he never mentioned what he encountered fighting the Japanese, but I knew by his silence that death was no stranger to him.

I remember he wrapped himself around me like a squid would wrap itself around its prey. We were both hot and sweating, but I didn't move. He may have not said much, but he didn't have to. Just being in the safety of his embrace spoke volumes. Death's darkness was conquered by my father; I wasn't afraid of dying anymore. This night was never mentioned again because my first encounter with death's darkness was rebuffed by my father's light.

This presents an interesting by-product. I have never been afraid of dying since that night with my dad. Have I been scared? Yes. I have been in a few situations I thought were life-threatening. Am I fearful of the process of dying? Yes. But I am not afraid of dying. I am not fearful of what is on the other side because of my faith in Jesus the Light.

Now here is another point to ponder. Normally, young children develop a fear of death because of attending a funeral, having a pet die, or losing a relative to sickness or accident. But in my case, my fear came out of nowhere. There was no life event that led to this fear. So what was the trigger? I don't know to this day and I don't think it matters. What does matter is that the external darkness of death breached the shores of my innocent, carefree life.

It was darkness beyond my ability to cope. So whether from fear of death or another type of darkness, a child needs a light to chase away the darkness. If he doesn't have this light, or if his fear is not addressed, a pattern will develop where he's not able to cope with any darkness encountered.

Darkness Exposed

Who or what is this darkness? From where does this darkness come? Why do we have to face this darkness? What is its mission? Why do we choose it over the light? Is it possible to avoid the darkness? Why does it become so comfortable? These questions have haunted me for thirty years as a counselor. In the following paragraphs I suggest some possible answers.

Let us start by asking, who or what is the darkness? I believe it is both who and what. Let me explain. As a Christian I believe the father of all lies is Satan. I believe he is also the father of deception, denial, treachery, suffering, pain, and every other torment humans have endured since Adam and Eve fell from grace and were promptly ushered out of the Garden of Eden. As counselors we often encounter clients who are in a desert time in their lives, and while in their desert, they want to blame God for all their ills.

"If he is all that loving, why is he allowing this pain in my life?" The correct answer is to redirect the blame for the pain experienced. God did not put the first couple in an imperfect Eden; he placed them in a precursor of heaven. It wasn't a blueprint or a first draft, it was the real deal. There was no pain, suffering, hunger, thirst, sickness, or disease. These afflictions did not exist until Adam and Eve bought the lie fed to them by Satan. He appealed to their human pride. They bit the fruit and went downhill from there. Why? Because Satan successfully appeals to the darkness of our human pride, and we have been blaming God ever since. We refuse to accept responsibility for our own darkness in which we've placed ourselves.

Now that we know the source of darkness, let us find the answers to our questions about its nature. The seven lessons to follow detail how to avoid the trap of temptation's darkness.

Lesson One: Satan can only tempt us if we allow him.

Satan cannot cover us in his darkness if we do not allow ourselves to be drawn into it through temptation. The issue then becomes not why did God allow this to happen, but rather why did I allow myself to be drawn into Satan's darkness? Personally, I don't believe Satan causes misfortunes, nor do I believe they are tests. We live in an imperfect world of natural laws set into motion after the fall in the Garden. Therefore, the darkness that envelopes us is a result of allowing ourselves to be drawn into Satan's trap of blaming God because we don't want to accept personal responsibility.

Satan is like a magician of sin on the stage of life and death. He distracts our attention through pain, and with deception in his right hand and a lie about who caused the pain in his left, he tricks us into believing it's all God's fault.

Lesson Two: We know we are embracing Satan's darkness when we do it.

That's right. No one tricked us. No one tied us up and forced us to embrace his darkness. We knew it before, during, and after we embraced his darkness—just like Adam and Eve knew. What was Adam's reply when God asked him why he ate the forbidden fruit? "Yes, God, I take full responsibility for my actions. I knew what I was doing was sin but I chose to ignore your law, and I ask humbly for forgiveness. Finally, as the head of the family, I take full responsibility for Eve's actions." Ha!

This was not his reply. Instead he said, "The woman you gave me, she gave me the fruit." Talk about selling someone out! But this is exactly what we do every time we play the darkness blame game. Everyone else is responsible for our actions.

Lesson Three: We need to be honest with ourselves about what is drawing us into Satan's darkness.

Temptation is not sin; it's how we respond to temptation that leads to sin. Temptation is part of life. We commit two sins, though, when we choose to deny we're facing temptation. First, we commit sin by lying to God that we are not being tempted. Second, we commit sin by lying to ourselves that we are not being tempted. When we commit these two sins, Satan has us hook, line, and sinker. All he has to do is reel us into his darkness. Being honest with God first and ourselves second is powerful stuff. Without this dual lie, Satan has no leverage.

Lesson Four: Acknowledge the struggle between the flesh and the spirit.

Pride is our enemy that blocks us from following this step. We don't want to admit this weakness, much less the need for help. This human frailty is exactly what Satan counts on.

If David had done this, would he still have sinned against God by committing adultery with and murder because of Bathsheba? If Judas had done this, would he have betrayed Jesus? The scriptures clearly point out from Genesis to Revelation that our struggle is not against flesh and blood but against the spiritual forces of Satan's world. And since this is true, we need all the help we can get.

Lesson Five: Give your struggle to God.

Yes, that's right. Give your struggle to God. This acknowledgement does not mean we stop being accountable or responsible. The fact we admit the struggle is beyond our scope and give it to the One who alone can handle it is being both accountable and responsible. Is this not what a child does when faced with a trial beyond his ability? Does he not turn to his daddy? In the same manner, we need to give our darkness to God, the heavenly father.

Lesson Six: Distinguish between darkness that is self-inflicted or of nature.

Most darkness we face is the result of our flesh consciously drawing us into questionable circumstances. However, there are episodes of darkness which are beyond our control. For example, being notified of a terminal illness, being laid off from a job, or losing a spouse or family member to illness or accident are dark events imposed on us by natural laws and are beyond our understanding or control. But we can still follow the principle of giving the burden to God. From Genesis to Revelation there are countless events cited where God intervened, but there are others where He did not. God is in control of the *big picture,* which we cannot see. We have to have faith that, no matter what happens, He knows what is best, especially when it's different than what we expect or want.

Lesson Seven: "Pull a Joseph."

This is a slang expression meaning, "run the other way." He followed all seven steps listed here and in the end had to literally run away from Potiphar's wife. In the process he lost his outer cloak, was fired from his job, was blamed for attempted rape, and was thrown into prison. Boy, talk about doing what is right and still being betrayed! We all know that in spite of these obstacles, travesties, lies, and injustice, God looked after Joseph in the big picture. He brought Joseph to being second in power over all of Egypt. Imagine, a Jew over Egypt. Only God can do that. And only God can deliver us each from our darkness.

Now that we have seen how to live in the light and avoid the darkness, I want us to look next at why we prefer the darkness over the light.

"The people walking in darkness have seen a great light; on those living in the land of the shadow of death a light has dawned." (Isaiah 9:2)

"It was not by their sword that they won the land, nor did their arm bring them victory; it was your right hand, your arm, and the light of your face, for you loved them." (Psalm 44:3)

FOUR
Three Reasons We Choose to Live in the Darkness

Here is the truth—we humans prefer the darkness. I know this is difficult to swallow. I know you and I don't want to say this out loud, but it's true. Right now, what I am writing is probably making you feel uncomfortable. So let's get really personal. You are not just uncomfortable, but you are probably squirming in your chair and have decided to throw this book across the room. You never want to read those words again because they hit you in your gut.

We have difficulty admitting that we prefer sin over righteousness, evil over good, dishonesty over honesty, even the darkness of adultery over fidelity. Wait, what did you say? Yes, I did include infidelity. Some of my readers are either in the darkness of an affair or are contemplating one. And whether you are physically involved in an affair or contemplating one, according to Jesus the two propositions are one and the same.

You may ask, are you serious? Definitely, because where the heart is, the mind, body, and soul will follow. Think about it. Long before you purchased that car you just had to own, it was already in your possession. You dreamed about it at night and imagined you were in it during the day. You could feel that steering wheel in your hands and smell that new car fragrance. This is the same darkness that occurs in your heart before an affair.

Why did I call it darkness? Surely there's nothing wrong with purchasing a new car, right? You're correct, but what happens often in the decision of purchasing a new car is that the passion of ownership exceeds the logic of ownership. So we buy a car we can't afford, and soon we are robbing Peter to pay Paul and our personal finances are in disarray. Is this not what happens when people engage in affairs? Our passion exceeds our logic and the next thing we know is that we've broken our marriage covenant. Soon our personal, matrimonial, and family lives are a mess when divorce becomes the selected solution to infidelity.

Let's not stop there. There are a percentage of men reading this who have an addiction to the darkness of pornography, a problem they've had since they were adolescents. They will never forget their first *Playboy* or *Hustler* magazine. They will never forget the first time they found free porn on the Internet or snuck into an adult bookstore. There are husbands reading this who view porn on their personal computers and phones or on their computers at work—maybe even all three. There are others who get up late at night or early in the morning to sneak into a room and view porn in the safety of darkness.

Now let's go back to the ladies. There are a percentage of women reading this who have been diagnosed with chronic depression and are not on medications. There are others who have manic depression and use the darkness of alcohol or drugs to control it. Women in each of these two groups prefer to stay in the darkness of depression instead of stepping into the light of overcoming the shame and admitting they suffer from mental illness. They struggle to get out of bed every morning, feel tired much of the time, are moody, and never want to have sex with their husbands. In fact, having sex is the last item on the to-do list of any of these women.

Next, let's look at men who struggle keeping their tempers in check. When was the last time you flew off the handle? When was the last time you yelled and screamed at your wife and children so effectively that they were fearful for their lives? When was the last time you physically abused your wife and/or your children? Every time you lose control, do you hear the sound of your father's voice? Do you recall the stench of cheap alcohol on your father's breath and on his clothes? How many times as a child did you swear you would never be like him?

Then there is the introvert—the husband and father who rarely talks, but his wife and kids never know when he will explode. When he does explode, he says and does things he would never say or do to anyone else outside the home. After his explosion is over, he is very apologetic; but apologies aren't enough, for he did the same thing just two days ago. What happens to families of a man who behaves in this manner? The children isolate themselves by either staying away from home or hiding in their bedrooms where they feel safe. Wives live in constant fear, never knowing when their easily agitated husbands will explode again.

Sometimes a daughter nearing puberty will begin cutting on herself in places concealed from her parents. These cutting sites are usually inside the thighs or upper arms where clothing covers the scars. Cutting herself is the only way she has control over her life, as everything else in the universe of her home is collapsing. Mom and Dad are usually too preoccupied with the darkness of their own faltering relationship to consider her individual adolescent needs.

The topics I have addressed so far are those most often presented in counseling; however, I have one last issue to discuss in the marriage and family arena. In the past twenty years of counseling, I have found that about eight out of ten women have experienced some form of sexual abuse. Here is a generic description of what transpires. For some girls, the nightmare begins between age five to ten. Sometimes it stops just after puberty. Other girls experience the abuse at puberty and it continues until they leave home. Sometimes the abuse stops because the perpetrator moves away or the association between the victim's and perpetrator's families ceases, as most of the time perpetrators are either part of the extended family or close family friends.

The abuse is rarely reported and, when it is, often nothing is done about it. So here are some questions these poor little girls are faced with for the rest of their lives. Don't I matter? Is there something wrong with me? Why was I touched there? Why was I forced to do those things? It's not difficult to analyze why they are usually in abusive relationships and have several failed marriages later in life. No matter how old these women were when they came for counseling, every one still contended with gaping psychological wounds. The darkness is not so much in the abuse they suffered but in the denial that it occurred. No one allowed the light of truth and healing to be shown to them.

I want to offer one last potential topic of darkness: marriage. Has your marriage been what you thought it would be? When did the dashing white knight become the black knight and when did Maid Marion become the Wicked Witch of the West? How long after the wedding did your interest in sex begin to wane? Six months? Nine months? A year? Was your wedding night a disaster? Has sex in your marriage fallen down to the bottom of your list of intimate encounters?

Has it been easy to live in the darkness of marital unhappiness? Do you feel like there's an iceberg between you and your spouse in bed at night? Do you wonder what that handsome stranger you saw at the PTA meeting would be like in bed? Have you mentally undressed that cute young girl who lives across the street who is young enough to be your daughter?

But I'm a Christian, you say. Yes, you may be a Christian, but you are still human. You were created in the image of God with the healthy and holy desires He placed in you. The trouble is that since Adam and Eve's fall we humans really don't know how to manage them.

What about the decaying relationship between a husband and wife? We often choose to ignore the situation by thinking it will improve on its own. Has this plan been successful so far? Since this strategy has not worked, I would like to offer three reasons why we choose to live in the darkness.

One: We Stop Seeking the Light

I have developed a series of questions for the first session of each new client in counseling. Several decades ago I noticed an obvious pattern in regard to the light's role in each client's life. It seems the light no longer was considered an important part of their lives, much less the foundation.

This pattern began to show that without the light in their lives, these people tended to make poor choices. Their decisions were not based on solid moral and ethical grounds but on whatever emotions they were experiencing at the time. These initial unhealthy decisions led to more bad decisions so that, eventually, their lives were in chaos. I began to give the absence of light in their lives different terms, such as a spiritual hole or spiritual emptiness or spiritual vacancy. These nontechnical descriptions were made not in judgment or criticism but merely to provide a vehicle to understand the absence of the light in their lives.

Living in the light is about relationship with the light. If we want to start living in the light and stop living in the darkness, we have to make that first big choice—the choice to live in the light instead of the darkness. This is a very tough decision because we have been away from the light for a long time.

This is just one of the many beauties of living in the light. The light does not care. The light's only concern is to have you back in its glow. It never stopped reaching, never stopped sending its invitation. It knew we felt a sense of defeat and knew the dark had convinced us the light no longer cared.

So how do we return to the light? One day at a time. Forget about why you left it. Let the light embrace you with its love and, like making amends with an old friend with whom you have had a falling out, spend time basking in its acceptance and forgiveness.

Two: We Stop Consulting the Light

Wait a minute, this statement doesn't make sense. If we have stopped seeking the light, then surely we've already stopped consulting the light. Let me ask you a question. Do we abruptly stop seeking or consulting the light? No, both are gradual.

Let's go back to the Garden of Eden. Do you think Eve succumbed to the serpent's first temptation to eat the forbidden fruit? I don't. I believe the deception occurred over an extended period of time. I have no proof, nor do I know how long it took before Adam and Eve crossed the line and disobeyed God. But having worked with people over the years, I've discovered that nearly every time they give in to the temptation to leave the light and follow the darkness, it is not an impulsive or spontaneous decision. (*see special note at the end of the chapter)

Just like in today's world, I think the serpent first approached Eve in a subtle, private manner, almost as if the proposition of disobeying God was not mentioned. I think it was more like a thought that popped into her mind. "Hey, why can't we eat this fruit? What makes it so different?" Perhaps these and other questions had crossed her mind many times. Then she viewed the abundance God had provided throughout the rest of the Garden and dismissed the question.

Satan didn't have to say any more. The seed of perdition germinated, grew, and took root, and soon Eve began hanging around the forbidden tree. She probably inched up to it several times, but then her conscience forced her to run away. However, each time she visited the tree she drew a little closer until, finally, she homed in on the fruit like a sniper looking through a scope. I don't believe she just ran up to the tree one day, grabbed the fruit, and took a bite. I think she might have admired from a safer distance the color, shape, and smell. Perhaps she sniffed the fruit hanging from a branch. Finally, when her courage to sin became overwhelming, she took the big risk.

Eve reached out and touched the fruit at first ever so softly. Aha. She didn't die! So she graduated to the next level, giving the fruit a slight tug. Still nothing happened. But she wasn't brave enough in her first romance with sin, so she ran home and waited until the next day. Early in the morning, when the light of day was just glimmering over the tree tops, there was Eve gazing helplessly at the fruit. The morning chill made her shiver—or was it sin's embrace?

I'm still torn about what happened next. Did she slowly raise her arm and extend her hand, wrapping it around the fruit? Then, like pulling out a loose tooth, did she gently wiggle its stem back and forth until it finally broke? Or, like a mouse darting across a kitchen floor aiming for a piece of cheese on a mouse trap, did she shoot her arm out quickly for her treasure? Which of these two final acts of her entrapment by sin caused her to eat of the forbidden fruit? Either way, she took the fruit from the tree, ate of it, and saw that it tasted good.

Is this not what happens to us today? Sin tastes good. It is an immediate joy and pleasure, but its enjoyment has an eternal consequence. As Adam and Eve discovered, the very first time we start tempting the flesh with any forbidden fruit is when we stop consulting God. How do you think Eve felt when she and Adam walked with God in the cool of the day while she was in an adulterous affair with sin? She probably felt the same way any of us do when our walk with God becomes tainted with secret sin and our guilt stops us from consulting God, our Light.

Three: We Put Ourselves First

When does sin occur? Is it in the act or the thought prior to the act? We all know the thought comes first, but I think there is a step before the "thought." I believe sin occurs the moment we dethrone God and enthrone ourselves. We literally take the crown from His head and place it on ours. When this happens, and not a moment before, we become vulnerable to the darkness. If we don't dethrone God first, then the "thought" of sin and the resulting action of sin won't follow.

Let's go back to the Garden. Look at the conversation between God and Adam. When God asked Adam why he'd bitten the fruit, he answered, "Eve, the woman you made for me, gave me the fruit to eat!" (Genesis 3:12) It seems comical because nowhere is there a written record of Eve twisting his arm, holding him down, and forcing him to eat the fruit. Adam thought by blaming Eve he would be off the hook. But he wasn't. His response demonstrated he had been wearing God's crown for quite some time.

We are all vulnerable to what happened to Adam and Eve. Therefore, in the next chapter I want to offer suggestions on how to find the light and keep it.

*Special footnote

I realize that in the Genesis account of Adam and Eve's temptation Satan makes only one proposition. I am not a Hebrew scholar, but I have worked with many people over the years and have seen that temptation usually occurs in the way I described it. Anyone may argue that it happened exactly as described in Genesis, and I would not stand in their way. In fact, I would bow to their scholarship. My attempt is to read between the lines and describe human behavior, which I believe has not changed since the Garden.

"You, O Lord, keep my lamp burning; my God turns my darkness into light."
(Psalm 18:28)

"The commands of the Lord are radiant, giving light to the eyes." (Psalm 19:8)

FIVE
The Triangle of Light: Making the Light Your Home

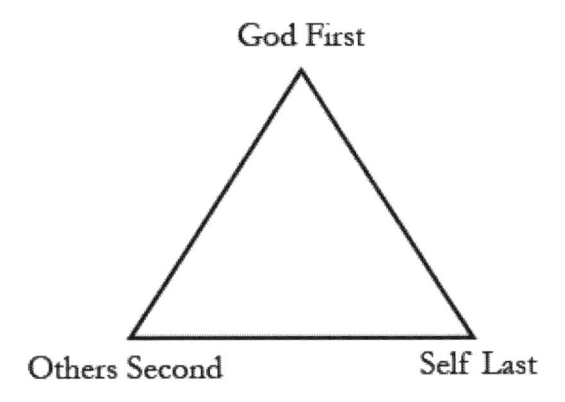

```
         God First
            /\
           /  \
          /    \
         /      \
        /        \
       /_____\
  Others Second   Self Last
```

I want to tell you a true story that illuminates the triangle of light illustrated above. When I was a medic in the Rhodesian army over thirty years ago, I met a man who was a Seventh-day Adventist. I'll call him Tom. He was not a pastor, missionary, or elder in his church but was just a regular guy and a self-taught mechanic by trade. He had his own business with a good reputation in the Bulawayo business community.

I was inspired when I first heard of his reputation. Tom served as a chaplain's assistant but found that this was not meeting his spiritual need to serve. The chaplain to whom he was assigned had the idea that in order to be accepted when he visited men in the field he had to take along *Playboy* magazines. My soon-to-be friend didn't want any part of this activity, so he asked to become a noncombatant soldier.

Now here's where his sainthood glowed in my mind. As a Seventh-day Adventist, Tom did not believe in working on Saturday, but he was flexible. A soldier cannot request special privileges when on the battlefield, so Tom proposed that he would go on patrol like every other soldier but that he would become the patrol's personal two-legged pack mule. His proposal was accepted.

He volunteered to carry extra ammunition, food, water, or anything the patrol needed and made no request for an exception for his case. He believed that as a citizen he was obligated to serve in the army, even though it violated his moral principles. So he served and made no special mention of it, nor did he request any recognition. I can't recall exactly because it was over thirty years ago, but I think he signed a legal document absolving the military of responsibility in case he was killed or wounded.

Tom was a quiet man, but when he spoke his words merited attention. One evening he and his wife came to our home for a meal. I was so inspired by his humble conversation that I decided to be a medic and not carry a weapon. I also submitted a document stating that I would not hold the Rhodesian military accountable if I were killed or wounded.

My friend's example illustrated the triangle of light depicted at the beginning of this chapter. How did he make the light his home? He put God first, others second, and himself last. There's only one way to consistently follow this triangle of light: we have to be honest when we examine our motives.

An Explanation of Self-Honesty

No one likes pausing long enough to look intently into a mirror. In fact, we will stand in front of a mirror for only as long as it will take to comb our hair, brush our teeth, shave, pluck our eyebrows, and so forth. Then, as quickly as we see our self-image, we vanish from before it posthaste. Yet it's precisely an intense examination in the mirror, an honest evaluation about what we see, that is required for us to change our image and, in turn, our lifestyle. But how do we do this? What does it mean to practice brutal self-honesty? The following paragraphs answer this question with a true story.

Several years ago I counseled a couple who were swingers. For those who are not aware of this lifestyle, it is a married or cohabiting couple who have an open marriage. This couple who came to see me had not intended to become swingers. He wanted to experiment, and although she was accommodating, she was not committed to this lifestyle. When their marriage started falling apart, they finally sought counseling. They had small children and the husband's business was collapsing. Although I could not convince him to admit it, the consequences of his lifestyle negatively impacted his business acumen and skills.

Like any addiction, swinging became this couple's lord and master, demanding fidelity in every aspect of their lives. Financially, they were living in a delicate bubble of pretense. They appeared the glory of success to family and friends, but they lived in financial hollows. Their marriage and personal lives were always on the edge of collapse. Neither of them trusted the other and each lived a lie of suspicion and doubt. When their parents realized what was happening, they decided to help them by paying for counseling.

At the end of our first session I gave the husband an assignment. I suggested he purchase a small spiral notebook and pencil and keep them accessible at all times. It was to be his thought diary. He asked what this term meant and I explained. I told him I wanted him to write down every negative, bad, evil, and immoral thought that would pass through his mind for the next week. I further explained that at our next session we would review his notes.

When he entered my office a week later the expression on his face was beyond description. He had tears in his eyes as he slumped into the couch across from my desk. He mumbled as he wiped away his tears, "I did what you requested and I am disgusted." When I asked why, he related that barely a thought had traveled through his mind that was not vile. He had sexual thoughts most of the time and could not contain the ugliness that filled his mind.

Sad to say, this was the first time in his young life that he had monitored his thoughts. Not only had he never monitored them before, but he had never attempted to stem their tide. They had become like a typhoon at sea. His vile thoughts tossed his insatiable libido in multiple directions without consequence or recourse. Even if he did put on the life preserver of decency and self-discipline, he was going down in his Titanic of unbridled lust.

Our next course of action was for him to not just examine every perverted thought but to learn how to expel these thoughts before they took up residence. Accordingly, his next goal was to start filling his mind with pure thoughts. He could accomplish this goal by abandoning any former behavioral practice that led to personal or electronic association of a vile nature. Accountability to his wife was a practical daily routine to ensure he was faithful to his new morally pure lifestyle. When he returned home each evening he was to give his phone, iPad, computer, or any other electrical device to her for inspection.

Men and women alike cannot venture down the road that allows the light to fill their lives until they eliminate hidden agendas and false motives, no matter how small. Not everyone reading this passage is a swinger, but there is a common battle we all fight—allowing the darkness in the world to enter our lives, even if it initially seems innocent and harmless. In order to safeguard our existence in the light we need to examine every thought daily and take it captive for the light. With this idea in mind I ask the reader to create a thought journal. Keep a little spiral notebook and pencil with you. Jot down every thought you have for about a week, and then ask how the darkness may have overshadowed the light in your life.

"I will set before my eyes no vile thing." (Psalm 101:3)

"You have set our iniquities before you, our secret sins in the light of your presence."
(Psalm 90:8)

"Light is shed upon the righteous and joy on the upright in heart." (Psalm 97:11)

SIX
Can We Really Know Another's Darkness: Inclusive and Exclusive Darkness

A Darkness Suggesting

I want to introduce you to a young girl of about fourteen years of age. She is sweet and innocent, on the brink of flowering into young womanhood. It is a magical time when she is both a little girl playing with dolls and a young woman who can charm any man by casting her feminine spell over him.

Gloria—not her real name—came for therapy because she complained of not being able to sleep at night. When I probed deeper into her story, I learned the reason. It seems she would see the shadow of a dark male image hovering in her room, first at the foot of her bed, then next to her side, and finally near her pillow. She couldn't distinguish the facial features but could tell by its dark outlined silhouette.

When I asked if this male shadow had a name, Gloria replied no. When I asked if others existed along with him, she again replied no. Her mental health deteriorated to the point of suicide. I suggested to her mother that Gloria should be entered into a local psychiatric hospital. During her week in treatment and medications, the male shadow retreated and Gloria could finally sleep at night.

After being discharged from the psychiatric hospital, Gloria came to see me for a follow-up visit. During our time together I was dazed by something she shared—she had been reading a Satanic bible. For some reason she had not thought it important to tell me prior to her hospitalization. I pressed for details and she admitted that this male image had not appeared until after she had begun reading it. Finally, she confessed that her inability to sleep had never occurred prior to reading her newfound Satanic bible.

When I asked why she would read a Satanic bible, she told me her mother had given it to her. This statement surprised me, so I asked her mother to join our session. When asked the motive for giving her daughter a Satanic bible, her reply was rather startling. She said she wanted her daughter to be unbiased about all faiths by having equal exposure; that way she could decide which faith, if any, she would adopt. I asked her to strike a bargain with me—she could keep her co-pay if I could keep the book. I still have this bible in a drawer in my office in my home today.

I wish to use this story as a setting for my next segment on defining more in depth both internal and external darkness.

How Darkness Comes into Our Lives

Our personalities are molded by the thoughts, feelings, conclusions, and decisions we make about life. These experiences form our rules and values and set our personal boundaries with individuals, groups, and society at large. They also lead to our cosmology; for example, what, if any, decision have we made about God and His existence? This decision will in turn influence our relationship with Him and our daily lives.

If we are not vigilant, darkness will cloud and overtake each of these aspects of our being. Gloria was innocent and vulnerable, and the Satanic bible obviously negatively impacted her internal light. Was the dark male figure she saw real? Was it her imagination? The answer is unimportant because either way his presence was real to her. Had we not intervened, Gloria may have committed suicide. However, once the Satanic bible was removed from her life, the dark figure and her depression disappeared.

Six Core Dimensions of Light and Darkness

I believe there are six core dimensions of personality that can be influenced by either the light or the darkness. Like a potter's clay, these traits are malleable. How we choose to model them determines the brightness of the light or the depth of the darkness.

One: Our Imperfect Sin Nature

All humans, no matter their education level, age, or personal enlightenment, share a common darkness—a struggle between the flesh and the spirit. Some people will argue this battle is between what we want and what we ought. Or, it can be expressed as a conflict between seeking immediate gratification and delayed gratification. The darkness of being human is not bad or evil; rather, being human means learning how to distinguish between what is right and wrong and then seeking to do right. The problem is that as humans we are more inclined to pursue evil over good because of our imperfect sin nature.

Two: Personal Struggles

Each human faces a daily struggle in seeking to do right over wrong—the struggle of the imperfect sin nature. This struggle can be a simple, easy choice requiring little thought. Or, because of personal internal justification or perceived-as-valid rationalizations, it could be a major, life-altering decision that causes a person to act narcissistically.

Three: Guilt

As humans we suffer regret and shame for making bad decisions. This guilt can come in two forms. First, the guilt can be healthy because a rule, principle, or virtue has been broken. The second is an unhealthy guilt due to having been forgiven but not yet forgiving ourselves.

Four: Limitations

No matter what our education, experience, or expertise, we are limited by our human imperfection at physical, emotional, psychological, and spiritual levels.

Five: Perceptions

We cannot escape the fact that, no matter how objective we try to be, we are influenced by our personal life experiences as being part of a family, culture, society, nation, and religion. Perceptions, whether our own or those of others, are not dark by nature but sometimes produce dark results and implications.

Six: Spiritual Orientation

A relationship with God, or lack thereof, influences mental health. There is a positive impact when there is a relationship and a negative impact when the relationship is damaged, in decline, or nonexistent.

Now that you have a better understanding of light and darkness, I'd like to pose a question that will be answered in the next chapter. Is it possible for one person to comprehend another person's light and darkness?

"The unfolding of your words gives light; it gives understanding to the simple." (Psalm 119:130)

"Wisdom will save you from the ways of wicked men, from men whose words are perverse, who leave the straight paths to walk in dark ways..." (Proverbs 2:12-13)

SEVEN
Transcending Darkness: How to Understand Another's Darkness

I want to introduce you to Mary (all the names in this chapter are aliases). Mary is about twenty-five, single, and lives and works independently. But she has a problem with anger, and because of it she keyed a car in broad daylight. She was sent to me for counseling but not for anger management or for keying the car. She was required by the court to attend counseling because she claimed she didn't key the car, but Bill did. Bill is not a friend but another person who lives in Mary as an alternative identity. In the first session Mary did all the talking because Bill refused to discuss keying the car with me. But she did know why Bill keyed the car. He was jealous of Mary's boyfriend.

During the second session I was introduced to Tom. Tom, like Bill, was a second alternative personality who lived inside Mary. It also seemed that Tom and Bill didn't always get along. They rarely talked with each other and both focused on talking to Mary independently, avoiding each other. Tom and Bill refused to talk with me no matter how politely I requested, so if they had anything to say they would tell Mary, whom they used as their medium. Sometimes I could tell when I was talking with Mary that one of these two alternative personalities was talking with her while she and I were conversing.

There are many other details about this case that are interesting but not important to this study, so let me conclude this case by saying I saw Mary three times. Were Bill and Tom genuinely part of a multiple personality in Mary? I will never know, but she was deeply troubled and I learned through her mother that she did have to pay a fine and repair the damage done to her boyfriend's car.

A Deeper Look into Inner and Outer Darkness

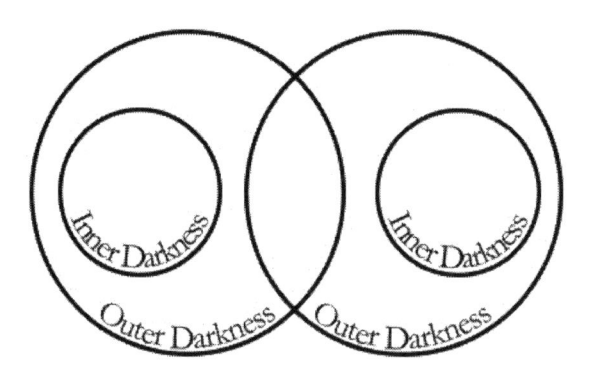

I now want to build on the concept of inner and outer darkness as previously discussed, first through the story of Gloria, the young girl, and then through the story of Mary and her alter egos, Bill and Tom. From these two stories I want to offer three traits about inner and outer darkness and three principles to follow to reach a client's darkness.

Three Traits of Inner and Outer Darkness

First, darkness between two people is simultaneously mutually inclusive and exclusive. Examine the circles above. You can see that no individual's inner darkness can be known by another. Thus, they are mutually exclusive, but the fact they are from the same culture makes them mutually inclusive. The degree to which they are mutually inclusive depends on the degree they share the same family, socio-economic society, culture, and language. Obviously, their mutual understanding will be influenced by how close they are in these and other aspects of being human.

For example, I'm able to understand Mary's psychosis as I have worked with psychosis before, although I have neither psychotic nor multiple personalities.

Second, outer darkness is not mutually shared. Two people may share the same or a similar threatening situation but not experience it in the same manner. This is because each person's inner darkness is unique. For example, Mary must have had some severe childhood experiences that led to her creating two alternative personalities in order to cope with her trauma. However, I have counseled women with childhood experiences of equal severity as Mary's who did not develop multiple personalities.

Third, the outer darkness is not equally shared. In my work as a therapist I have noticed that when children come from stable, supporting homes, they tend to manage life's outer darkness better than children who come from unstable homes. Another interesting observation is that those who had been raised in stable homes manage life's darkness better as adults than those raised in unstable homes.

Principles for Therapists to Follow to Reach into a Client's Darkness

First, a therapist can never fully understand a client's darkness. There is a tendency with counselors to say "I know how you feel," as a means of identifying with the pain in the clients' stories of darkness. But there is no way counselors can accurately make this statement even if they have suffered in the same type of dark experience. The reason is that no two people can suffer the same darkness and share it in the same manner, even if it is at the same time.

Second, the client cannot fully understand the counselor's darkness. For the same reason a counselor cannot grasp a client's darkness, neither can a client grasp the counselor's darkness.

Third, a therapeutic connection is achieved as the counselor attempts to leave his or her darkness and explore the client's darkness. There are several principles of therapeutic connection between therapists and clients that I wish to share. First, as discussed earlier, a counselor can never fully explore a client's darkness. Second, at best, a counselor can offer to attempt to cross over from personal darkness into the client's darkness. Third, the ongoing effort of transcending the boundary between the two separate aspects of darkness is more important than the degree of success or failure of crossing over. Fourth, as each attempt is made in successive sessions, the counselor will benefit as much from the experience as the client will, gaining new insights in life about personal darkness as well as the client's darkness. Fifth, it is a herculean effort to try and leave behind one's own darkness and attempt to enter a client's darkness, often resulting in surprising results.

Now that we have the tools necessary to reach into another human being's darkness, I would like to proceed to the next step in helping others with their darkness.

"Wisdom will save you from the ways of wicked men, from men whose words are perverse, who leave the straight paths to walk in dark ways, who delight in doing wrong and rejoice in the perverseness of evil, whose paths are crooked and who are devious in their ways. (Proverbs 2: 12-15)

"The path of the righteous is like the first gleam of dawn, shining ever brighter till the full light of day. But the way of the wicked is like deep darkness; they do not know what makes them stumble." (Proverbs 4:18-19)

EIGHT
Sharing Light and Darkness: How to Help during Dark Times

One of the conundrums we have to face is that we don't all agree on what is light and what is darkness. What some of us consider darkness may be someone else's light and vice versa. Terrorism existed in Rhodesia three decades ago like it does today in much of our world. Many terrorists who participated then thought they were living in the light, as do many today. I lived with terrorism thirty years ago and still have some association with the subject today through my work.

However, I still cannot see the light in laying land mines, ambushing innocent civilians, and murdering women, children, and babies. The only way I can see any light at all is by accepting that there are varying shades of white. For instance, how can light of any shade place a civilian in a grass hut, block the door and windows, and then set the hut on fire? How can there be any light in burning a man to death while laughing at his screams?

SOULAR ECLIPSE

How can light enter a church mission in the pitch-black night, seize the only two white couples, and drag them out of their homes? How can light, no matter what shade, take the husbands and torture them to death in front of their wives? Furthermore, how can light take one of the women, who is pregnant, and cut the baby out of her stomach while she is alive and then murder the other woman while she is begging for mercy?

I have asked myself these questions for over thirty years. These are not events I witnessed firsthand, but they were reported and confirmed by the news and by comrades-in-arms in the Rhodesian army.

One event I did witness firsthand occurred when a patrol returned after being out for several days. In their sojourn they came across a small village where an old, blind African man and his two younger wives lived. The terrorists claimed these people were traitors to their light and had to teach them a lesson. They stripped them down and cut off the right buttock cheeks of the old man and his youngest wife, who happened to be four months pregnant.

I will never forget the expression on the face of the medic who accompanied the Rhodesian soldiers, both black and white alike, who carried the old man and his wife on rigged stretchers. It was a very hot day and they all were sweating profusely. They had carried the two wounded civilians a long distance. As the stretchers passed by I noticed the old man and his pregnant wife were lying on their stomachs, displaying large bandages that covered the areas where their right buttock cheeks had been severed only hours earlier.

The medic stared at me, his face as white as a ghost. It was almost as if he'd seen an extraterrestrial being. And really, he did see something outside of his world experience. He was the one who saw where the right buttock cheek had been cut off, nearly to the hip bones, on these two innocent, harmless civilians. He opened his mouth and half stated, half asked, "I didn't know what else to do?" He had covered the wounds with antibiotic ointment and then placed large chest-wound bandages over them, which were the only items he had that would cover the size of the injury area.

These terrorists had clear consciences. They didn't have to justify their actions because what they did was part of their light. Darkness to them would have been if they had not tortured these two civilians. So the definition of what is light is relative. I don't write this statement as a way of concession but as acceptance of a universal truth.

Having laid this foundation, I want to propose a vignette of shared light and darkness. In it I want to offer what I think are the means by which we can cross from our light and darkness to others' light and darkness.

Existential Vignette

Imagine you are in a pitch-black room. Your eyes are wide open, but you can see nothing in the darkness. While groping for the light switch, you bump into another person who is just as lost as you. Together you seek a common solution for escape. Then, the two of you find a single match on the floor and excitement fills you both. This one small match is your salvation; you can now find your way out of the dark room. You scratch the match across the rough, dry floor and are momentarily blinded as the illumination of its white and red flames pierce the blackness that once held you and your companion captive. Then, with this brief glow, the two of you quickly find your way out of the darkness.

Counseling Metaphor

I believe the next vignette describes the counseling process of both the therapist and the patient. In my opinion, both the therapist and the patient are equally lost in their own unique darkness. The difference between their shared but separate darkness is that the therapist has found the match—therapeutic skills—which is the means to point the client toward the exit from darkness.

What Does it Mean to Find the Light?

The light of an epiphany, the *aha* moment of an enhanced awareness, is like the flame of a match when first struck. It burns with a bright red and white glow. The counselor uses this flame in the darkness to guide the client to a deeper understanding, which will enhance appropriate change. However, this same flame of new understanding equally enlightens the counselor as it offers light in his or her own darkness. It may not be a light the counselor specifically needs or wants at this given time, but it still remains a light. Either way, both the therapist and client benefit.

Triangle of Skills to Help Others

Know and Understand Your Own Darkness

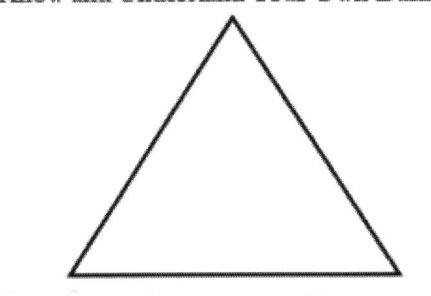

Acknowledge and
Resist Your Darkness

Be Transparent About
Your Darkness

I think the first skill set you need in order to help people in their darkness is to *know and understand* your own darkness. By this I mean you have to recognize how your darkness impacts your life and relationships and accept that you can only fulfill certain behavioral objectives in helping others.

The second skill set you need is the ability to *acknowledge and resist* your darkness. It means I have to overcome the fear that just because I have personal and professional weaknesses doesn't mean there's something wrong with my emotional and mental health. My darkness is real and is a burden, but it's not an anchor. My darkness does not need to slow down my desires, ambitions, and dreams. My darkness does not mean I'm dysfunctional. The more accurate I am in acknowledging the depths and boundaries of my darkness, the better I am able to contain its negative impact.

The third, and most difficult, skill set is to be *transparent* about your darkness. Some people feel that if they acknowledge their darkness openly it will detract from how others will view them. I have met many people in a variety of walks of life who openly confess their temptations, addictions, weaknesses, and mistakes. It seems that the more transparent they are, the more people are drawn to and trust them. They lead by their weakness because acknowledging it becomes their strength.

NINE
Questions about Our Own Darkness

Now that we have examined the eternal struggle each of us faces between our personal light and darkness, how do we make sense of it? How do we bring it all together to not only see our own darkness but also help others? How do we ignite that flicker on the tip of the match that burns bright enough to give us that epiphany?

I believe there are eight questions about our light and darkness that address these issues. If we are willing to conduct a close self-examination, then the darkness will lose its power over us as it submits to light. Let me say at the onset that answering these questions and facing these truths is no easy task, nor will facing the truths be accomplished in a few sessions of self-discovery. Instead, addressing these eight points will be an ongoing life struggle fraught with success and failure. However, each day we seek to grow we will have less darkness and more light in our lives.

Eight Questions

1. What's at the heart of my darkness?
2. What has formed and shaped my darkness?
3. How deep am I willing to probe into the depth of my darkness?
4. With whom am I willing to share my darkness?
5. Is there a door to my darkness I am afraid to open?
6. How honest am I with myself about my darkness?
7. How do I hide in my darkness?
8. Why do I hide my darkness?

"This is the verdict: Light has come into the world, but men loved darkness instead of light because their deeds were evil. Everyone who does evil hates the light, and will not come into the light for fear that his deeds will be exposed. But whoever lives by the truth comes into the light, so that it may be seen plainly that what he has done has been done through God." (John 3:19-21)

TEN
Merry-Go-Round of Darkness

Alright Glenn, now that I have read your previous chapters, what's your point? All your stories are helpful and I can see the struggle between light and darkness, but what does this have to do with me? In fact, I can think of more questions for you. What did you want me to gain from exploring this eternal struggle between light and darkness? Is there a central theme or thesis? And finally, what does this have to do with any change in my life?

I'm glad you asked, because I want to tell you about a spider in my office that will bring everything together.

Itsy, Bitsy Spider on the Wall

One day recently, as I was trying to think of a way in which to wrap up this book, I noticed a spider on a wall in my office. First, he crawled a little vertically, then horizontally, then down a little bit, then he backtracked a step or two. Not once did he abandon the wall and drop down to the floor or any other surface with his thin white silk.

My itsy, bitsy spider made a circumference of the room in about an hour. In fact, he was on his second lap when I began to track his progress, so I watched this spider continue on his second journey. Then I got busy again, and by the time I left my office I think he was on his third or fourth journey. Not once did he stray off his beaten track, as though he was on a spider super highway.

Can you guess what I saw on the wall the next morning when I came into my office? You're right, my little spider friend was still in his quest to circumnavigate my office. He'd obviously been thwarted in escaping my office because the door was closed and I have no window.

Itsy, Bitsy Spider and Me

So Glenn, what does this spider have to do with me? As I was driving home and thinking about this spider's pointless journey, several ideas of the struggle between light and darkness occurred to me.

First, every human being lives in the middle of an eternal spiritual war between the light and darkness over mankind's ultimate spiritual destiny. "Our struggle is not against flesh and blood, but against the rulers, against the authorities, against the powers of this dark world and against the spiritual forces of evil in the heavenly realms." (Ephesians 6:12)

Second, like my little spider friend we confine ourselves to the darkness of our own limited little world. In it we circumnavigate within our finite understanding, and the darkness becomes comfortable.

Third, what if I tried to befriend my spider interloper by picking him up in a paper cup so I could transport him outside the room to freedom? What would he do? He would run and hide. In his eyes I am a colossal being who is beyond his understanding. Is not God's light beyond our full understanding? And like my desire to help my spider friend, does He not reach out in the light of His Son to help us in spite of our ignorance? And don't we run the other way for the same reason?

By the way, that spider is still lost in my office. Are you still lost in darkness or have you found the light? Like my office, we have a door, and the light stands on the other side knocking. Go find that match, strike it, and let it lead you to finding this door so you can reply to the light's request to enter your life.

ACKNOWLEDGMENTS

There are three men who are not only my bosses but my friends of whom I feel honored to say they continue to inspire me, Daniel Conti, Tim Sumiec and Sam Warren.

Our two children and their spouses are a daily inspiration to me, Colleen and Jason Lee and Kirk and Minerva Goree.

There are two friends who read and offered valuable suggestions in the earliest drafts of this book, Lew Lambert and Michael White.

Melissa Ortiz runs the departments of counseling and community outreach at our church and I would be remiss if I did not publically thank her for keeping my life in order.